100 Simple Truths all Virtual Assistants Should Know

ISBN: 978-0-9995632-0-5

Edited by Hannah Batty, Sandi Garoutte and Ariel Kostrna
Cover & Layout Design by S. Audrey Isbell

Printed in the United States of America.

AVA Virtual Assistance, LLC.
1867 Williams Hwy, Ste 207
Grants Pass, OR 97527
541-244-2606
www.AVAPowerUp.com

100 *Simple Truths all*
Virtual Assistants
Should Know

S. Audrey Isbell

Introduction

To be a stellar VA and administrative hero, you've got to be willing to "face the truth". Truth in the experiences. Truth in the emotions. Truth in the technology. On and on, we discover the realities of what I call "VA-dom" and learn to navigate them with as much wisdom as we can.

Several years of building my practice had me wishing for a close VA buddy with whom I could talk to at length about work – knowing that they would fully understand or at least laugh with me over ridiculous things. I hope that these 100 simple truths I've discovered help you or at least make you laugh. When you find yourself wishing for a VA buddy, who could discover weird, good or bad truths, reach for this book and take comfort in its pages.

Sometimes we get truth and wisdom from others. Sometimes we discover simple truths for ourselves ...and in that case, I have reserved some pages of this book just for you. Enjoy!

My simple truth today is this...

_____

_____

_____

_____

_____

_____

_____

_____

_____

_____

_____

_____

_____

_____

_____

damn, that's good!

1

You can learn more about the world through a single Client's perspective than you ever thought possible.

My simple truth today is this...

damn, that's good!

2

Technology will always demonstrate its ability to serve up a new kind of challenge.

My simple truth today is this...

damn, that's good!

3

Some people want to use Virtual Assistance as their "get rich quick" scheme.

My simple truth today is this...

_____

_____

_____

_____

_____

_____

_____

_____

_____

_____

_____

_____

_____

_____

_____

damn, that's good!

4

Online business professionals must work twice as hard at communicating with others.

My simple truth today is this...

damn, that's good!

5

No matter how much love and care you put into the work and professional relationship... Clients still break up with you over email.

My simple truth today is this...

damn, that's good!

6

You will have to get out of that chair and meet people...in person.

My simple truth today is this...

damn, that's good!

7

Optimal performance of tasks will greatly depend on a Client's foresight and ability to plan ahead.

My simple truth today is this...

damn, that's good!

8

Clientele who already know and succeed at delegation are ideal.

My simple truth today is this...

_____

_____

_____

_____

_____

_____

_____

_____

_____

_____

_____

_____

_____

_____

damn, that's good!

9

You don't have to know everything, you just have to be willing to learn.

My simple truth today is this...

_____

_____

_____

_____

_____

_____

_____

_____

_____

_____

_____

_____

_____

_____

damn, that's good!

10

You don't have to do the work that's painful. Refer your Clients to an expert in that field.

My simple truth today is this...

_____

_____

_____

_____

_____

_____

_____

_____

_____

_____

_____

_____

_____

damn, that's good!

11

People acknowledge your
effort best when *you* do.

My simple truth today is this...

damn, that's good!

12

It's always best to take ownership of your mistakes and help resolve them with a positive attitude.

My simple truth today is this...

_____

_____

_____

_____

_____

_____

_____

_____

_____

_____

_____

_____

_____

damn, that's good!

13

Time off from work is best without a phone and computer.

My simple truth today is this...

damn, that's good!

14

Everyone deserves to know
what's expected of them.

My simple truth today is this...

damn, that's good!

15

Finishing something before you start another thing will help you stay inspired.

My simple truth today is this...

damn, that's good!

16

It's common sense to know that some days you'll feel productive and some days you won't. Prepare to feel frustrated regardless.

My simple truth today is this...

damn, that's good!

17

Taking the time to get organized will relieve stress.

My simple truth today is this...

damn, that's good!

18

You already know far more than you think you do.

My simple truth today is this...

damn, that's good!

19

You will get spontaneously nervous talking to people about what you do, even on days when you're feeling most confident.

My simple truth today is this...

_____

_____

_____

_____

_____

_____

_____

_____

_____

_____

_____

_____

_____

damn, that's good!

20

Your website is never "done".

My simple truth today is this...

_____

_____

_____

_____

_____

_____

_____

_____

_____

_____

_____

_____

_____

_____

damn, that's good!

21

People and potential clientele will take you even more seriously when you don't work from a home office.

My simple truth today is this...

damn, that's good!

22

Clients will treat you how
you've taught them to.

My simple truth today is this...

_____

_____

_____

_____

_____

_____

_____

_____

_____

_____

_____

_____

_____

_____

damn, that's good!

23

Referring people to other VAs
now and then will benefit you.

My simple truth today is this...

damn, that's good!

24

TV or a good book will help take your mind off of work.

My simple truth today is this...

damn, that's good!

25

Neither Captain Kirk nor Sheldon Cooper will defeat your heavy workload. It'll still be waiting for you when you return.

My simple truth today is this...

damn, that's good!

26

Breaks are helpful but not entirely necessary.

My simple truth today is this...

damn, that's good!

27

Sleep is a non-negotiable.
Being a Virtual Assistant
doesn't make you R2D2.

My simple truth today is this...

_____

_____

_____

_____

_____

_____

_____

_____

_____

_____

_____

_____

_____

_____

_____

_____

damn, that's good!

28

You will forget to drink water.

My simple truth today is this...

damn, that's good!

29

Completing a one-time project can lead to more sustainable work.

My simple truth today is this...

damn, that's good!

30

Carefully reading and carefully responding to correspondence is imperative to success.

My simple truth today is this...

damn, that's good!

31

Someone always thinks that
you should do it their way.

My simple truth today is this...

damn, that's good!

32

Most of your time will be spent on things you never anticipated doing.

My simple truth today is this...

damn, that's good!

33

Too many people will ask for your help and expertise without expecting to provide payment in kind. Communicate your boundaries.

My simple truth today is this...

damn, that's good!

34

Asking for referrals will
sometimes make you feel dirty.

My simple truth today is this...

damn, that's good!

35

Procrastination is best left out of your vocabulary.

My simple truth today is this...

damn, that's good!

36

You can't be everything to everyone. You may have to grow your practice/team to delegate or choose to let some existing responsibilities go.

My simple truth today is this...

damn, that's good!

37

You'll learn to recognize and hopefully celebrate both large and small accomplishments often. Primarily to help maintain your sanity.

My simple truth today is this...

_____

_____

_____

_____

_____

_____

_____

_____

_____

_____

_____

_____

_____

_____

damn, that's good!

38

You don't have to work under pressure, just because you work well under pressure.

My simple truth today is this...

_____

_____

_____

_____

_____

_____

_____

_____

_____

_____

_____

_____

_____

damn, that's good!

39

There is a different industry for helping the technologically challenged.

My simple truth today is this...

damn, that's good!

40

People will jokingly ask if you are "virtually there" (with them). The first time you hear this, you'll be amused... the billionth time, not so much.

My simple truth today is this...

damn, that's good!

41

Having a passive income strategy is no excuse for keeping with an unsustainable business model. Figure out a profitable service offering.

My simple truth today is this...

_____

_____

_____

_____

_____

_____

_____

_____

_____

_____

_____

_____

_____

_____

damn, that's good!

42

You truly can work from anywhere, providing you have a working computer, internet access and are 100% paperless in everything you do.

My simple truth today is this...

damn, that's good!

43

You will consume garbage thinking it educational, at least a few times in your career.

My simple truth today is this...

_____

_____

_____

_____

_____

_____

_____

_____

_____

_____

_____

_____

_____

_____

_____

_____

damn, that's good!

44

Holding yourself accountable is perhaps the single most important characteristic for you to have in order to be an "A List" Virtual Assistant.

My simple truth today is this...

damn, that's good!

45

Getting discouraged comes
with the territory.
"Put on some big girl panties
and get back to work"
~ a truly wise woman

My simple truth today is this...

damn, that's good!

46

It's foolish to not have a backup of your computer data.

My simple truth today is this...

damn, that's good!

47

You don't have to be a
bookkeeper, but you'll do well
by having your bookkeeping in
order.

My simple truth today is this...

damn, that's good!

48

Nothing lasts forever. Even your best, deep-relationship, Clients, will one day move on.

My simple truth today is this...

_____

_____

_____

_____

_____

_____

_____

_____

_____

_____

_____

_____

_____

damn, that's good!

49

You will perform harmless tasks you've already advised against.

My simple truth today is this...

damn, that's good!

50

You won't always have the skill needed, prior to saying you can do the work.

My simple truth today is this...

damn, that's good!

51

Failure is *not really* what you're afraid of.

My simple truth today is this...

damn, that's good!

52

You will want to work all the time. Don't.

My simple truth today is this...

damn, that's good!

53

People don't always know
when your confidence is down.
You will, but they won't.

My simple truth today is this...

damn, that's good!

54

Other people's expectations will weigh heavy on you. Set good boundaries early.

My simple truth today is this...

damn, that's good!

55

You will forget to stretch your body. Alarms are helpful in this case.

My simple truth today is this...

damn, that's good!

56

You'll never learn how to manage your time, but you can learn how to practice time management.

My simple truth today is this...

damn, that's good!

57

Free apps are useful in the beginning.

My simple truth today is this...

damn, that's good!

58

Setting prices based on what you think others can afford is a mistake.

My simple truth today is this...

_____

_____

_____

_____

_____

_____

_____

_____

_____

_____

_____

_____

_____

_____

damn, that's good!

59

You can be selective about your clientele and still turn a profit.

My simple truth today is this...

damn, that's good!

60

You'll be surprised at just how many of your Clients don't keep or use a business plan.

My simple truth today is this...

damn, that's good!

61

Most administrators are undervalued and underappreciated. VAs who don't verbalize the smallest wins will fit that mold as well.

My simple truth today is this...

damn, that's good!

62

Cell phone notifications will make you think about work at the most inconvenient times. Priority notifications help to resolve the issue.

My simple truth today is this...

damn, that's good!

63

Your marketing analytics only work well for you when you set goals and review data on a consistent basis.

My simple truth today is this...

_____

_____

_____

_____

_____

_____

_____

_____

_____

_____

_____

_____

_____

_____

_____

damn, that's good!

64

If you're resourceful, you can serve Clients no matter the operating system. Mac vs PC makes little difference.

My simple truth today is this...

damn, that's good!

65

Asking the right questions can save you a ton of time when completing a project. You can even ask an A.I. bot (Artificial Intelligence).

My simple truth today is this...

damn, that's good!

66

Working on your VA business will energize you and push you to keep going, so don't sell all of your time to Clients.

My simple truth today is this...

damn, that's good!

67

You will discover that (despite your best effort) some people just won't understand what you are trying to tell them.

My simple truth today is this...

damn, that's good!

68

Phone and email interruptions will destroy a workday. Best to have a plan around that.

My simple truth today is this...

damn, that's good!

69

Awesome VAs make a commitment to ongoing education early.

My simple truth today is this...

damn, that's good!

70

It's "old school", but writing down all the things you've been worrying about will help you feel and work better.

My simple truth today is this...

damn, that's good!

71

You don't have to grow your VA business into anything larger than what makes you happy, and profitable.

My simple truth today is this...

damn, that's good!

72

The work you're given isn't about you, it's about your Client and their success. So, don't forget to ask for testimonials.

My simple truth today is this...

damn, that's good!

73

You'll have to monitor your own addictive behavior. When you take a peek at your email, you've just gone back to work.

My simple truth today is this...

damn, that's good!

74

You can reduce liability to yourself and others by requiring a secure method for sharing passwords. LastPass is highly recommended.

My simple truth today is this...

damn, that's good!

75

Nevermind comparing your VA business to any other. Skill sets differ, and your own uniqueness is your best U.S.P. (unique selling proposition).

My simple truth today is this...

damn, that's good!

76

WordPress might be your favorite web platform, but it's still beneficial to be familiar with others.

My simple truth today is this...

damn, that's good!

77

Your Clients will remember when you were last out with a terrible cold. Take care during cold/flu season. Your ability to work is memorable.

My simple truth today is this...

damn, that's good!

78

You won't regret investing in a standup desk option early on. This goes for ergonomic keyboards and mouses too.

My simple truth today is this...

damn, that's good!

79

You will have great ideas about how to run or change your VA business that nobody else seems to agree with.
Try them anyway.

My simple truth today is this...

damn, that's good!

80

You don't have to "sell" people on what you know they already need. Sell how YOU fulfill the need.

My simple truth today is this...

damn, that's good!

81

Being virtual doesn't excuse
you from "being present".

My simple truth today is this...

damn, that's good!

82

What you take time to appreciate is what you value.

My simple truth today is this...

damn, that's good!

83

Marketing material that's "original" doesn't mean that others won't display their originality the way you do.

My simple truth today is this...

damn, that's good!

84

Sometimes you just need to ask Google if there is a way.

My simple truth today is this...

_____

_____

_____

_____

_____

_____

_____

_____

_____

_____

_____

_____

_____

_____

damn, that's good!

85

Reacting to email only makes you "busy"; it doesn't mean you are getting something done.

My simple truth today is this...

damn, that's good!

86

You will be led to believe that you must have a passive income strategy in order to remain in the VA industry.
It's not true.

My simple truth today is this...

damn, that's good!

87

Yes, you do need contracts.

My simple truth today is this...

_____

_____

_____

_____

_____

_____

_____

_____

_____

_____

_____

_____

_____

_____

_____

_____

damn, that's good!

88

Electronic searching methods are quicker than physically searching for what's lost, so get those paper files digitized.

My simple truth today is this...

damn, that's good!

89

Virtual businesses that provide certainties to their Clients & prospects will have a much easier time with retention.

My simple truth today is this...

damn, that's good!

90

Sharing what you know, is only pretentious, if your delivery implies that you are never wrong.

My simple truth today is this...

_____

_____

_____

_____

_____

_____

_____

_____

_____

_____

_____

_____

_____

_____

damn, that's good!

91

SEO (Search Engine Optimization) can be improved by taking the time to appropriately name the files you upload to the web.

My simple truth today is this...

damn, that's good!

92

Sometimes you will want to work late. Avoid setting this precedent with your Clients, schedule messages/email to send on the next business day.

My simple truth today is this...

damn, that's good!

93

You will want to attend conferences and invest money in your own education; this is why budgets and planning exist. Make it happen!

My simple truth today is this...

damn, that's good!

94

VAs are often treated better than traditional administrative professionals. There doesn't seem to be a good reason for this.

My simple truth today is this...

damn, that's good!

95

Public speaking is a fact of life for entrepreneurs. The virtual assistant industry is no different.

My simple truth today is this...

damn, that's good!

96

Project and task management requires willingness to communicate during all phases of the work.

My simple truth today is this...

damn, that's good!

97

People don't always hear you
the first time when you make a
recommendation.

My simple truth today is this...

damn, that's good!

98

Being desperate for work limits your potential. There is plenty of admin work in the world.

My simple truth today is this...

damn, that's good!

99

Typos happen. They are not the end of the world...not even for your Client.

My simple truth today is this...

damn, that's good!

100

Being thoughtful is a surefire way to be memorable. And since VAs work remotely, being memorable is perhaps twice as important.

My simple truth today is this...

damn, that's good!

www.ingramcontent.com/pod-product-compliance
Lightning Source LLC
Chambersburg PA
CBHW071148050326
40689CB00011B/2020